24 Day Challenge

To Living Uncuffed

CAPRICE SMITH

ISBN-13: 978-1494299293

ISBN-10: 1494299291

DEDICATION

This challenge is dedicated to my husband and four
amazing sons who sacrifice so much so that
I may follow my dreams.

ACKNOWLEDGMENTS

I am very grateful for the support and direction of my mentor Rodney Hill.

TABLE OF CONTENTS

Caprice Smith is a writer that writes from her heart. By telling her phenomenal story, she addresses the reader at their inner most self. In sharing her most vulnerable moments, Caprice gives you the opportunity to feel the realness of who she is, where she has come from, and what she overcame to become the strong empowering woman of God she is today.

Growth and change comes at a cost. The deeper the change, the greater the cost. The question is: how much are you willing to pay to become a better you? Because the cost can be great, most people choose to remain stagnant in their lives, never wanting more for themselves. For some it is easier to stay in a place of hurt and pain because that's all they have known for most of their lives. To move from that negative place to a place of healing and empowerment means that you have to pay the cost of facing that "thing." The "thing" that keeps you from reaching your purpose. In this book, Caprice shows you how to confront your past and not allow it to dictate your future, by simply sharing her story. She walks you through those moments of change in her life where she tackles her fears and overcomes them by facing them head on. Essentially, pulling those deep rooted weeds from its source to lay down a foundation for fertile ground and the bearing of good, positive fruit.

Through her own growth and healing process, Caprice developed a strategy to help other women in pursuing their purpose. Caprice empowers, motivates, and strengthens other women to move towards their calling with an unwavering zeal. As a coach, she provides you with the tools and resources needed for your business to become successful. As you read her story, Caprice draws you in and connects with you on a level deeper than surface. She reaches a place in you that will impact your life in such a way, that you will absolutely want to go after what you want in life.

As a great business coach, a great public servant, a great wife and mother, but most of all, as a great woman of God, Caprice Smith has impacted the lives of others through her continuous efforts of creating "SharperMinds", and by building on a niche that pushes people to only strive for their best.

Juliet Jones

1 INVOLUNTARY DETENTION

I believe there are strong empowered people who still feel like they are missing something, but deserve to embody a have it all, balanced life.

A big step toward truly honoring your distinctiveness is to claim your purpose. Many people get stuck in a rhythm of going through the motions and forget to nurture their drive. This *24 Day Challenge to Living Uncuffed* will help you understand the connectedness of your persona and the path of your creative expression. The purpose of this *24 Day Challenge to Living Uncuffed* is to provide a glimpse into the life you could have when you gain balance, discover your unique purpose and truly live free of emotional baggage, displaced guilt and unwarranted shame. Everybody has a very distinct purpose, but only a few people actually fulfill their purpose. You can be included in the minority, but the self work has to be completed first. Otherwise, you may find yourself mimicking others. Unfortunately, when you try to take on someone else's purpose, you feel unbalanced.

When an individual is arrested, the arresting law enforcement officer has twenty four hours to either criminally charge them or release them from their custody. That rationale is utilized in the *24 Day Challenge to Living Uncuffed*. By the end of this challenge, you will have made a decision to live free and will no longer be confined to the bondage of your own mental handcuffs. You will live more empowered, free and happy. Through intense self reflection and a series of strategic exercises, you will identify what has been holding you back and eliminate that element.

Law enforcement officers are taught to rely on clues to solve crimes. You will be taught how to interpret the clues and latent messages of your life so that you live empowered and liberated. You only need an open mind and to be completely honest with yourself in order to unleash your personal greatness. As you take this journey through the *24 Day Challenge to Living Uncuffed,* enjoy the ride! As

5

you read you will observe excerpts from Uncuffed~ Behind My Smile and easy to follow guidance. Things do not always have to be difficult to yield results.

Is your life balanced?

Are you doing things enthusiastically?

Have you gotten lost in everyone else's priorities?

Do you know what your purpose is?

If you answered pessimistically, than you have made a good decision to take the *24 Day Challenge to Living Uncuffed.* Through your voyage, you will be ushered through several phases and emerge renewed, with a clear focus on your life.

Noticeable Results

- Your communication style will be improved, because you will better understand your purpose and confidently share it with the world.

- You will be happier, because you will have freed yourself from the bondage and baggage of your past, consequences of poor decisions and other's perception of you.

- You will be different, friends and family members may need a little adjustment to get use to the new you. It may be a good idea to encourage them to take their own journey.

Let's get started today. You deserve to live the life that you were called to live. The *24 Day Challenge to Living Uncuffed* is composed of sections designed to show you the relationship between your personal experiences and your inner joy. It is also designed to teach you how to secure your path to real happiness and self confidence. Most of all, it will teach you how to honor your uniqueness, live empowered and balanced.

You may already do the things that you really enjoy, like parenting, your career and volunteering, but the *24 Day Challenge to Living Uncuffed* will help take things to the next level.

Why Now?

The bigger questions is why not now? Aren't you ready for a BIG change? Are you ready to be uncuffed?

Do you really maintain the same level of passion for the things that you enjoy over time, or do they seem like chores after a while? Do activities take on a personality of their own leaving the impression that you have lost control of them? Has the normal routine of juggling work, family and self become chaotic? Do your personal goals change daily? Do you find yourself constantly starting and stopping ventures? If so, the great news is that in twenty four days, you will not feel that way. The old layers will have fallen off and you will have new wings to soar. Your colleagues will be astonished by the new version of you. The fresh new way that you leave your impression on people will be undeniable. You will learn secrets that take others a life time to learn. The only requirement is that you complete each step in succinct with the next. Try not to move through the chapters out of order, because the flow will be interrupted and you may miss critical points. Also, understand that your level of growth depends on your level of commitment. No one can do the work for you. Lastly, there is no cookie cutter solution that fits everyone. So, make this challenge special to you.

Days 1-2

Challenge: *You are challenged to live with the innocence and purity of a child for two entire days.*

Like many, my innocence was damaged as a child, but even so I rewrote my story as an adult. By completing the necessary work on myself, I stripped away repression. I claimed power over everything, my past, present and future. The self work has to be completed first. You were once blameless and full of dreams, you can go back. This is just one thing that I had to contend with.

Excerpt

...the fact that I had the darkest complexion out of my siblings didn't help much. They would always tease me and tell me that I was black and ugly with big lips. I just pretended it didn't bother me even though their taunts and teasing picked away at my self-esteem. I truly believed I was the ugly duckling. I remember watching a new movie with flying monkeys, I believed I was looking in a mirror. This was my negative self-perception until I was around twenty-one years old. Failed relationships would reinforce this negative self-perception.

Was your innocence impacted negatively? Do you have poor self perception? Embrace your inner child. Who did you want to be when you grew up? Yes, "who" and not "what" did you want to be? The world's teaches us to live within boundaries of things that are proper and rationale, but there is a child inside screaming to mess things up. So, why not get dirty? Break up your routine, learn to dance or even paint a picture. Try something new, it will jilt the inner child and give you an opportunity to enjoy yourself. Ever been to a gun range? Learning to shoot is really exciting, just please seek a professional trainer before handling any weapon. What about singing? We probably all wanted to be superstars, start your singing career. There is always karaoke.

Try this.

Close your eyes and slow your breathing. As you take breathes, imagine the last time you laughed so hard that you felt like you would burst. If you can't remember, it has been way too long. If you can recall an instance, stay in that moment. While you are there, imagine that you are holding a mirror. Now, look at yourself. Aren't you beautiful when you are happy? Are you ready to re-create that moment, or design a new moment filled with happiness and playfulness?

There is an inner child in us all. Have you ever wondered why birds fly and fish swim? It's because of instinct. Likewise, humans desire to connect with other humans. The universe connects all of us on some level and we communicate intimately through instinct. Instinct has a way of calling us to action, just like the flying bird or the fish. That's why our intuition is usually right on. Identify that nagging feeling and respect it. If we keep silencing that nagging feeling, we stay in a place of just existing or settling, which is not necessarily a peaceful place.

We should recognize that anyone can be a person of greatness, if only they paid more attention to their inner voice. Hone in on what your inner voice is telling you and listen to it. Do something out of character and see what happens. You have permission, not to use your inside voices. Scream out loud, if it moves you.

The next time you get on an elevator, pay attention to the inner voice; it may cause you to move just a little slower to think about your safety. Go ahead and get use to the sound of it; you will eventually recognize it more quickly. Also, try to identify your first thoughts of the day? Are you thinking about email or social media, your job, your family or something else? Try to be silent for the first four hours of your day and examine what thoughts you have. Write them down. Do this for two days and you will have gained insight about your inner voice. You will also be more honest about what moves you and what's nagging at you. This is a step toward getting unstuck and making your greatness happen quicker.

Days One-Two Assignment

At the end of each day, answer these questions by jotting down the first things that come to mind in the spaces.

Answer these questions:

1. Who did you want to be when you grew up? Yes, "who" and not "what" did you want to be?

   _____

   _____

   _____

   _____

2. The world's teaches us to live within boundaries of things that are proper and

rationale, but there is a child inside screaming to mess things up. So, why not get dirty. Think of three ways to break up your routine.

_____

_____

_____

_____

_____

_____

3. Map out the first few things you do each day.

    a.

    b.

    c.

   d.

   e.

4.   Identify your inner voice.

   a. Describe it:

   b. Is it masculine or feminine?

   c. Is it positive or negative?

   d. When do you hear it the most?

   e. How   often   to   you   follow   the

      instructions of your inner voice?

Questions	Day 1	Day 2
What did it feel like when you first noticed your inner voice?		
Was it difficult to obey it at first?		
What childhood memories did you have while reading the excerpt?		
Whose voice did you hear during the exercises? Were they motivating you or telling you that you could not do it?		

Use this space to journal about your dreams as a child. Write about what you thought your career would be. Write about anything that comes to mind. What was your fondest childhood memory? What was your saddest?

_____

_____

_____

_____

_____

_____

_____

_____

_____

_____

_____

Notes Page

2 MISDEMEANOR

Days Three-Four

Challenge: *You are challenged re-invent one thing that has happened in your life.*

The thing about imagination is it can transform your mindset instantly. My twelve year old son wrote about imagination and it was awesome to read his perspective. You will need to use your imagination in order to complete this part.

Noah Smith wrote,

"IMAGINATION... My imagination can be like a door or a car. It can be like a door because I can open up my imagination and it will show me an infinite number of opportunities. I can open up as many doors as I want. When I open the doors I can choose where to go. And I can customize the doors however I want.

My imagination can also be like a car. It is always running and always active. But it can crash if I don't stay in the right lane. But when I am in the right lane it can take me where I need to go."

Understanding that you obviously will not literally go back into time and changed your past, but you can use your imagination to take you somewhere else. You will get a better understanding of that moment and discern which parts should be left behind. You will highlight the parts that motivate you. When you choose not to dwell on the past, you enable yourself to move on. When you re-design your past through imaginative exercises, you gain control over it. Remember the key is not to eliminate the past, but to draw on the positive. You are in control over everything about you, even your past. At least you are in control over the level of impact that the past has on you.

It took me a long time to learn this piece. As a child, I appeared on a local television show and missed the winning question that cost my academic team the win. It was so awful at the time, but today

I laugh about it. I have since used my imagination to focus on the humor instead of the embarrassment.

Excerpt

A small group of us from Westport Elementary School traveled to the studio. The set looked a lot smaller in person. The red and blue furniture did not seem as bright when I stood right next to it. There were about six of us selected to represent the entire school. It was a gleaming moment. We each had a chance to answer questions and even made it to the second round.

The school we competed against was from a neighborhood filled with home owners and two parent, non-dysfunctional homes, or so it appeared. They knew all the answers, but we were in the game. The score was tied and it was all on me. The emcee leaned over toward me and calmly asked me to name the building in the picture on the screen. There was a picture on the screen and all I had to do was tell the audience what was in the picture. It was a picture of the World Trade Center. However, since I had never left my neighborhood I had no idea what the screen showed."

Days Three-Four Assignment

Pick two of the worst moments of your life and re-design them. Use the following pattern.

Who was present?		
What happened?		
How were you impacted?		

At the end of each day, answer these questions by jotting down the first things that come to mind in the spaces.

What moment did you remake?	
Why was it important to you?	
What did you change?	

Use this space to journal about the remake. Make it as interesting as possible. This is important, because you will have re-written your life. Soon, positive memories will replace the other ones.

_____

_____

_____

_____

_____

_____

_____

_____

_____

_____

Notes Page

3 SURVIVOR'S UNIT

Days Five-Six

Challenge: *You are challenged to live in the moment as it's unfolding.*

Many people never take the time to be kind to themselves. People miss many opportunities to live in the special moments and enjoy the fruits of their labor. For instance, instead of celebrating very productive work days, they grow frustrated that more tasks were not completed. It is not uncommon for them to bring home these sentiments and jump into other ventures, without taking a break. This type of pushing can bring about fatigue and a loss of patience. Being overwhelmed negatively impacts personal relationships. Make today the day you reward yourself. Pauses are great in life; give yourself a chance to de-clutter your mind. Get creative about ways to be quiet. Be still long enough to hear your inner voice that will guide your next steps. Make today the day that you honor your uniqueness, live empowered and balanced. Live in the moment. When I sang publically for the first time, I was definitely living in the moment.

Excerpt

I spent a lot of time finding myself. I was driven to conquer the world, just was unsure how I would accomplish that. At one point I decided I was going to be a singer. Yes a superstar, I thought I could sing to. I put all my energy in practicing songs and sharing my voice to anyone who would listen. I even sang the message on the home telephone. I was very sure of my Grammy winning voice. I courageously entered into a local talent show. My mommy, Bob and Jeremiah showed up for my first talent show. I meticulously picked out my outfit; I had on black lycra and cotton shorts, sparkly black strappy platform shoes and a black and burgundy short leather jacket. My hair was straightened, with bangs cut in an Asian style and I had on cute make-up. There I was, my big moment had arrived. The curtains opened, slowly one panel slid to the left and the other to the right. I had my head held down with complete diva attitude. I slowly raised my head for a dramatic effect and started clapping my hands; this crowd was going to know I was the next big thing."

Days Five-Six Assignment

Think about the last event you planned, attended or participated in. Did you notice the smell of the day or the beauty in it? Well here is your chance.

Write about your moment; give as many details as possible.

My moment,

At the end of the day, answer these questions by jotting down the first thing that comes to mind in the spaces.

When was the last time you allowed yourself to be totally uninhibited?	
What did it feel like? Why did it end?	
Would you do it again?	

Use this space to journal about the moment.

_____

_____

_____

_____

_____

_____

_____

_____

_____

_____

_____

_____

_____

_____

4 OPEN CASE

Days Seven-Eight

Challenge: *You are challenged to create a ripple effect!*

It is interesting to see people attach themselves to posts in social media, they respond to all types of motivation and inspiration. It seems like the most simple post gain the most attention. I would share what I believed to be really insightful information and would not get a response, but when I lightened the message, there was overwhelming show of support. Have you ever received a huge level of support and were surprised by it. The unexpected times, that everyone loves something you said, but you didn't even think it was that great. They follow your actions, but you are not doing things for that reason.

Make a conscious decision to become the best you, then I promise you people will love and support the authentic you. Your uniqueness is important enough to be acknowledged. That means you can start today. Break the mental bondage that has been forcing you to live in fear and hesitancy and create a movement of your very own. Let's think about mental bondage. What things have left a lasting impression on you? Do these things cause you to say yes when you know you don't want to? Have you stunted your own growth by doing this? Do you get caught up in routine? Do you live every moment to the fullest? Starting today, enjoy YOUR life! Make your life's statement bold so that it vibrates outward just like a ripple effect! You have to make an effort for your brilliance to leave its mark on this world, or nothing will be totally rewarding and fulfilling.

When I competed in my first competition, I never expected to win anything, but I did. Apparently, I had made a big enough impression that created a ripple effect, leaving people wondering about me. You will do the same thing by the end of this *24 Day Challenge to Living Uncuffed.*

Excerpt

They announced the second runner up; Mrs. Texas graciously walked up and received her trophy.

Then they announced the first runner up; At this point, I stopped listening for my name. They said, "Mrs. Owings Mills." I was stunned and grew emotional. I was speechless, like when Porter proposed. I was shocked beyond belief. No way had I won first runner up, did they make a mistake? To them it was first runner up. To me, it was a triumph for my mother, Chloe, all the survivors in all the cases I worked, my boys and all my friends. I actually won first runner up. That was incredible. As I walked up to get the trophy, I replayed my award speech. The first runner up does not give a speech; not even the winner does. However, if I had not said my speech in my mind, I would have been immobilized. The crowd cheered and showed their love. It felt awesome, my face was beat red. Thank you lord! "He who began a good work in you...will be faithful to complete it," my favorite song played on and on in my mind. To many first runner up was no big deal, for me in my less than perfect wardrobe and half done nails, it was everything. When I walked off the stage, all the judges came up to me telling me my story was inspirational. They were so kind, but had not really heard my story. Up to this point, no one did.

Days Seven-Eight Assignment

Create an affirmation statement that you will recite every night. Let's get the abundance, success and greatness by first claiming it. Use this formula.

1. Write a sentence about who you are right now.

2. Followed by a sentence of who you were, when you were younger.

3. Then add who you will be.

Affirmation Statement

ex. I am a business coach and survivor of many things. I have overcome low self esteem and I am the first author to sell one million copies of her book on the day it was released.

_____

_____

_____

_____

_____

_____

_____

_____

_____

5 EVIDENCE CONTROL

Days Nine- Ten

Challenge: You are challenged to love yourself, so you can accept the gift of love from others.

Did you know that you already have what it takes to have an incredibly happy life and the power to build healthy relationships? Sometimes, we miss good relationships, because we get in our own way with unchecked emotional baggage. We tend to forget what makes us attractive to other people. Today, I challenge you to embrace the person that you have chosen to call your mate. If you are not dating, embrace yourself. It's funny, when my husband and I began dating; we discovered that we had both reached a level of frustration with the dating scene. If you are like me, the dating scene really just meant that you were making yourself available just in case that "perfect person" came along. Unknowingly, my husband and I arrived at the same state of frustration, at the same time. Was our meeting chance, was the universe aligning things for us or was it an act of GOD? One may never know, but the point is to be prepared when it comes. Our frustration prepared us to be ready for one another.

Ironically we should have met long before we actually did. We discovered that we knew all the same people and visit the same social settings. Fortunately, we met at a time when we were both ready for a meaningful relationship. Essentially we were READY for one another. This made things exciting and fresh. You can still get READY to make your current relationship fresh or find the one that you are looking for. For now, let us think about the recipe for a healthy relationship?

*Find a realistic model. Do not get caught up in making the same mistakes that your parents may have made or try to live that fairy tale dream. Keep in mind that things will not always be perfect, but you can practice until you perfect it. That means, if you like surprises, start surprising your mate or if you don't have one, surprise others. Send a co-worker flowers anonymously or buy lunch for a stranger. Being kind will become a habit. You can piece together a model from many sources. The important thing is to create your version and start modeling.

***Keep it fresh**. Start a routine doing the things that you like to do. If you like to read, join a book club. People are far more interesting when they do the things that they like to do. Do more than one thing that you find interesting. This will provide more topics to discuss with your mate or potential mate and keep things fresh. You may even surprise yourself about what you like.

*Jazz things up a bit. Imagine trying to catch a fish without a fishing rod or bait, yes it can be done, but it would probably be very difficult. As long as we have fishing rods and bait, why would you even want to try to catch a fish without the tools? Think of you mate or potential mate as the fish, why not add flare to get their attention? Try a different hair style or new perfume. Try to change the topics of your conversation. Change can be revitalizing. Have fun with it.

*Warning signs. This subject has been exhausted, so I will not waste time here rehashing everything to look for. The bottom line is, if it feels wrong, it probably is. Take notice and run for the hills if you sense that something is not right. In others words, just distance yourself from negativity, hostility and relationships that bring you down.

*Accept the gift of love. When you work through the aforementioned, you are more prepared to accept the amazing gift of love. You know that you are in a healthy relationship when you wake up excited to be in this relationship. You feel secure when other people are around. You feel empowered to be yourself and to love them. Lastly, you do not want to cling to this person with death grips, because you know they love you the same way. The best way to get this type of love is to accept yourself first. I had to complete the self work, before I could even recognize love. Are you the same way?

Excerpt

On this day, I was very tensed. Porter and I argued about something ridiculous, probably about the weather. We argued, because I thought he was intentionally making us late, again. I had never really gotten over him being late on my wedding day. I accused him of being jealous of my success; the one person that was always in my corner. I am still not sure why I made such a horrible accusation, but have regretted it every day since. He was in no way envious, but I was stuck in the mode of dysfunctional thinking, believing that life had to be hard, instead of easy and genuine.

Days Nine- Ten Assignment

1. Pay for a stranger's coffee.

2. Give someone you know ten dollars, for no reason.

3. Volunteer for one hour on one ministry at church or in your community.

4. Tell someone about how you created your affirmation statement, then show them how to create their own.

Use this space to journal about the remake. Make it as interesting as possible. This is important, because you will have re-written your life. Soon, positive memories will replace the other ones.

_____

_____

_____

_____

_____

_____

_____

_____

_____

_____

_____

6 PLAIN CLOTHES

Days Eleven-Twelve

Challenge: *You are challenged to settle your personal issues by training the way you communicate.*

Excerpt

The closer I got to police headquarters, the more excited I grew. The handsome mounted cop gave me confirmation that they allowed models on the police force. I walked into the double glass doors with my blue eye shadow and red lipstick, my long dangling earrings and a fresh attitude. I went to the front desk of police headquarters. "Are you guys hiring?" The older gray headed uniformed officer stared at me as if I had three heads. Surely, I was not trying to get a police job. I didn't look like a cop. In addition, I was far too happy to handle the streets of Baltimore, so he thought. He gave me a look that almost knocked down my confidence. Little did he know, I was prepared for this. I was used to having to prove myself. In my most professional voice with a stern voice, I looked at him square in the eyes and said, "Hello, my name is Caprice. Is the City Police Department hiring? I would like an application!" I could see my mother's face filled with pride and acceptance. I could see my daddy's face and imagined ways that I would have arrested him for all the wrong he had done. More importantly, I saw Chloe's face. She had endured so much, just so I would not have to. I needed to be successful for her, Jeremiah, my mother and Tae. I needed to be successful for me. No more being "poor, broke and hungry".

The gray haired gentleman handed me an application and told me to return on Saturday, when they would be administering the test. You would have thought that he handed me a million dollars. "I accept!" He looked at me, perplexed because he had not actually offered me the position. He had no idea about the self-affirming conversation that I just had in my mind. I chuckled and said, "I mean I will be here for the test." I gathered all of my documents and started exercising to get ready for the run. I was about five feet, eight inches tall and one hundred and twenty five pounds; not really out of shape, but I did not work out regularly and needed to prepare myself.

Women especially struggle with understanding how important their communication style is. The male receptionist had no idea of the personal struggle I had dealing with his response to my inquiry for a job application. However, his non verbal communication spoke volumes. Non communication is more powerful than the spoken word.

To communicate effectively, you have to understand who you are. Most people have uncomplicated desires; they simply want to know that they are important, accepted, and loved. While some people are little more complicated, they need to feel sexy, have security, and feel appreciated. People desire to be treated nicely. Moreover, they wish to be heard. Funny thing is these priorities change their order of importance almost daily. One thing that remains consistent is a person's need to be heard on an intimate level. When we talk, we want to know that someone is listening. The best way to get people to listen is to understand your personal communication style and match it to others.

Understanding others is essential. Do not treat everyone like they are your best friend, every conversation has to be customized. Men do not need to share as much as women do. Females are natural sharers and very willingly giving out information about many personal things. In fact, females are very open about what bothers them, what delights them, their dreams and even their darkest secrets. Cell phone companies have sold a billion phones, by relying on this very concept. They would agree that females spend more time talking and sharing, than they do spending time quietly alone self-reflecting. Dating partners are expected to understand us the most. Unfortunately, they are usually the ones who know the least about what makes us move. So chitty chat a little less with your friends about what they think about you and take the time to discover what you are really trying to communicate and to whom. Learn to connect with a person's soul. Try not doing all of the talking, just listen for a change.

In any relationship, parent/child, spouses, dating partners, schoolmates, co-workers and friends, there is a hierarchy of styles regarding communication, ranging from most productive to least effective. They are respectable conversation, silence, passive aggressive insults, debate and argument. There are several forms of acceptable communication; for instance, we nod our head in acceptance. We wave our hand as a way of greeting one another. We shrug our shoulders to demonstrate that we do not understand, we offer compliments to strangers, we write inspirational thoughts; the list is perpetual. Likewise, we

converse with one another in varying ways,

sometimes in loving traditions, sometimes in anger,

sometimes while crying and sometimes in a

whisper. Recognizing these various levels of

communication is key to how effective you

communicate with others.

Days Eleven-Twelve Assignment

Reflect on your communication style, which style do

you use the most?

_____

_____

_____

_____

_____

_____

Where did you get the style from?

Who do you most resemble when communicating?

Are you often asked to repeat yourself?

Do you always leave a conversation wishing you restated something?

Do you show confidence and demand respect when you communicate?

This is the most basic formula for effective communication.

---

1. Shoulders back, chin up and maintain excellent posture.

2. Check your emotions at the door.

3. Determine the purpose for having the conversation.

4. Launch the conversation with a greeting.

5. Listen while the other person is speaking.

6. Restate what you heard them say.

7. Pause before responding.

---

*Remember, what you say is never as important as what others think you said.

7 THIN BLUE LINE

Days Thirteen-Fourteen

Challenge: You are challenged to hit the re-set button in your life.

Recall what motivated you in the first place. Remember those resolutions that you made at the beginning of the year, it is time to bring them back to the forefront of your mind. Set your eyes on the goal and make it happen. One way to energize your life is to recall what motivates you. When you have the life that you love, you will automatically want to be present for everything that will happen in your life. You enjoy others and they enjoy you. Some people launch several projects, chasing that euphoric feeling of starting something new; this will also lead to burn out.

Instead of stretching yourself thin, master one thing and show others your passion about it. One way to invigorate yourself is to take care of yourself. If you don't reward yourself, you may grow resentful and before you know it, you will not want to do the things that you once enjoyed. Reflect on those New Year's resolution; now make some realistic ones. Try doing things differently and see if the results change. Every year I remind myself that I must help other women to find their voices, because I struggled to have one for so many years.

This motivates me to keep serving my purpose. What motivates you?

Excerpt

I was able to put up a theoretical wall in the room while speaking to groups. I was helping so many when I spoke publically, it was cathartic and rewarding. I would work between eight to twelve hours, get off of work, run home and organize my business. It was rewarding and fun. I met so many incredible women, who were stuck in the valley. I motivated them find their own purpose and serve the community. I put my mental resources to good use as I grew successful.

Days Thirteen-Fourteen Assignment

At the end of the day, answer these questions by jotting down the first thing that comes to mind in the spaces.

What motivates you?	
Why is it important to you?	
What old goals can you re-visit?	

Use this space to journal about the remake. Make it as interesting as possible. This is important, because you will have re-written your life. Soon, positive memories will replace the other ones.

_____

_____

_____

_____

_____

_____

_____

_____

_____

_____

8 BULLET PROOF

Days Fifteen- Sixteen

Challenge: You are challenged to satisfy your need for attention.

Shake up your daily routine. Get more satisfaction from your life by unleashing your need for attention. Express your opinions openly and gently, it will gain your peers respect, when they know you hold a position. Gain motivation from your inner voice. That means do what you enjoy doing and avoid doing the things that bring you less pleasure. Make a habit of spending quality time alone every day or every week. Then try to have a telephone conversation with a person that you have texted/ emailed in the past month more than three times. Sometimes, we get so caught up in the convenience of emails and texts, that we lose personal connections. We need these connections to satisfy our need for attention. It is a refreshing change for people to hear your voice.

Create opportunities by reinventing yourself, try by learning something new. Lifelong learners are happier, because they create opportunities to challenge themselves and make revelations. Write your life's story; include your dreams and aspirations. It can be a fun way to remind yourself of what moves you. If you already do these things, share them with a friend. One of the biggest decisions I ever made that would re-shape my life was shared with my mother.

Excerpt

I woke up the next morning feeling like I could walk on air, I was SUPER woman! My pseudo cap was flying in the wind, as I stood there with my chest puffed out and knees locked; ideas were bursting from my mind. For the first time in my life, I heard a happy song, an empowering song. I told my mother that I would take the test. We held hands and jumped up and down from excitement. I was determined to get what I wanted in life! I was looking forward to making more money and meeting my goals.

Days Fifteen- Sixteen Assignment

Write down your life's story. Yes I am asking you to write your autobiography. One page about your highlights; this is different from your affirmation statement, because you should only write the truth.

Autobiography

_____

_____

_____

_____

_____

_____

_____

_____

_____

_____

_____

_____

_____

_____

_____

_____

_____

_____

_____

_____

_____

Use this space to journal about the remake. Make it as interesting as possible. This is important, because you will have re-written your life. Soon, positive memories will replace the other ones.

_____

_____

_____

_____

_____

_____

_____

_____

_____

_____

_____

9 SHARPENED MIND

Days Seventeen-Eighteen

Challenge: *You are challenged to serve your purpose.*

In order to serve your purpose, identify the thing that you are constantly called to do over and over in every setting. I am often called to help & mentor women and teens at church, work or in general. Get this, I love doing it. You probably love doing what you are constantly called to do. Decide that you have a GOD given purpose that makes you special. Your message can only be given in YOUR voice, no one can say and do things exactly the way you can. So, go ahead use your outside voice. Give yourself permission to walk in YOUR greatness. That means, embrace your moments as they unfold. Being true to self is the first step to serving others. One way to serve your purpose is to discover what your message is supposed to be to the world. Start by putting your time and energy into discovering more about you. Write your story. Start a blog or do something that gives you power over your self-expression.

Excerpt

After you inspire yourself, examine your internal radar. I have said this many times before during a speech and truly mean it. "Listen inward." Rely on yourself. Become hyper about your needs, your emotional health, and all the good things about you. You have a message that can only be told in your voice. Be clear. Your purpose can not be fulfilled until you take the first step.

So now that you are all fired up and ready to walk in your purpose, do you know where you are going? What's your purpose? The big cue: WHAT's the point? In graduate school the "so what" factor is very important to research. If you are not making things better or different, what's the point? How are you impacting your community? How are you shaping your family? What's your point? Que es el punto tuyo? Stop minimizing your greatness to make others feel better. You must grasp the importance of your life.

I spent several years as a police detective and met many wonderful people. In that time, I made many accomplishments, like earning Unit citations, authoring a books and earning a Masters Degree. I am most pleased that I mentored several young adults and women. In the uniform, I discovered my niche of empowering women. I help them identify things that prevent them from being their best self and/or becoming entrepreneurs. Once the latent "thing" has been revealed, like a hidden fingerprint, my clients and I uncover their unique purpose. Everyone has something special that they must do in the world. Learning your purpose, that is the biggest gift you can give to the world.

Walk in your full greatness sometimes that means becoming an entrepreneur, sometimes it means volunteering; it always means feeling empowered and freed.

Destroy the purpose stealers called P&J. Try to clean from the inside out by tackling procrastination and judgment. You can literally change how successful you are and even how much money you make by giving yourself a make-over or in this case a "make-inner." Find the new version of you by doing these things,

Prioritize: We get bogged down with tasks that are distracting and over bearing, instead of doing things we truly enjoy. Start by making a list of the top five things that you enjoy the most. Then make it your point to do at least one thing on the list daily. You can easily accomplish everything on your list weekly. Eventually, you would have created habits of doing things that you love.

Affirmation: If you have not created an affirmation statement, make one right now. Recite it every day and night, until you have trained yourself to it. The Law of Attraction mandates that your positive affirmation will attract the positive things that you want. It is so easy to talk ourselves out of getting the things we want, but it takes courage and wisdom to seek the things you want.

Self Empowerment: Kick procrastination and judgment in the butt, they should no longer hold a place in your life. They both symbolize fear, in most cases the fear of success. When you conquer them, you create spaces for motivation and praise. It is your responsibility to yourself to live your best life, start today.

Okay, let's step back, before you go karate chopping P&J, you need to be trained. Use calendars to set deadlines. You can even set reminders, this should get rid of procrastination. Next, learn that perfection is for the Savior, you are only human and will not never obtain it. So, STOP trying, just be your best self. When you are your best, there is little room for judgment. Lastly, instill rewards when you accomplish small tasks. Soon you will doing back kicks and knuckle fist all over P&J.

As you move forward in your purpose, you must determine if the extension of you found within your book, your business, your ventures or your thing is aligned with your special purpose. Is it a mix-match? Some people are not successful, because they start things that do not match their unique purpose. It's not their fault; they often start ventures to fill a void in their lives or to make more money. These quick starts offer immediate gratification; unfortunately, quick fixes usually don't last. Before you decide to make your next move, think about where your passion lies.

Days Seventeen-Eighteen Assignment

Describe your purpose and determine your next move.

My purpose is

_____

_____

_____

_____

_____

_____

_____

_____

_____

_____

_____

_____

_____

_____

_____

_____

_____

_____

I know this is my purpose, because

_____

_____

I plan to serve my purpose by

These are the steps I will take to serve my purpose.

Describe the different steps you will take toward serving

your purpose.

Sample: My purpose is to start a non-profit to clean up the Chesapeake Bay.

Step 1

Research similar organizations.

Step 2

Organize a group of supporters to assist.

Step 3

Write out your mission and organizational goals.

Step 4

Establish a fundraising plan.

Step 5

Register with the state.

Step 6

Seek legal assistance to ensure legal compliance.

Your specifics steps should be projected up to twelve.

Step 1	Step 2	Step 3	Step 4	Step 5	Step 6
Step 7	Step 8	Step 9	Step 10	Step 11	Step 12

9 DEFENSIVE STANCE

Days Nineteen- Twenty

Challenge: You are challenged to identify obstacles early.

Trust that when you decide to live strong and empowered, obstacles will still arise that will distract you. There are key elements that you must pay attention to in order to continue to serve your purpose. You must be completely convinced that your purpose is both necessary and will be served in perfect timing. Many people lack dedication, launching your own venture without the right leadership and support can be tedious and overwhelming. If you jump into it, without realizing the amount of work involved, you may become fatigue. It takes a lot of dedication to continue to manage things, even when things are not looking the brightest. However, when it's your life's purpose, things are interesting and fun.

You also have to be aware that not everyone will understand how important your purpose is, especially family and friends. Negativity from others makes it very difficult to continue to nurture your drive. It is much more difficult to continue when everyone is telling you to quit. Sometimes, you just have to motivate yourself. Tune out negativity from others and follow your passion. Dig deep into your soul and know that the right people will show up to support you in perfect timing, when you choose to serve your authentic purpose. Remember you must serve your purpose, because there is someone else waiting on you so that they can be uncuffed. Look in the mirror and ask yourself, have you achieved all that you wanted to?

You may believe that you have eternity to find and serve your purpose; that there is plenty of time left to reach your dreams, but you could be wrong. Every day that you fail to tell your story or carry out the vision, is a day that someone else will stay stuck. They need you to do your part first. Start by following this formula.

No Street Signs!

Imagine driving in a town where there are no street signs. How in the world would you ever know where you were going. You probably though to yourself, that you could follow landmarks. Yes that is a good way to think, hopefully, none of those landmarks will change. It is better to have a clear path. Write out your goals and direction, make it plain. If it is too difficult for you to understand, it isn't clear enough. For example, if you wanted to start your own business, but are experiencing difficulty deciding what type of business you should start, you are not ready to start your own business. You may need to spend a little more time in the brain storming phase. Write out your ideas, so you can honestly evaluate them.

Then take the initial stride to make it happen. This may sound a little contradictory to step one, but you have to make the first step, even while perfecting the plan. There are many dreams that die with dreamers. Don't be a dreamer, tell a friend about your idea, write the business plan, research similar businesses and make it happen. Yep, every business first started by someone making themselves vulnerable, sharing their ideas and taking a leap of faith. You could be the next big thing. If owning a business is not for you, be the best version of you ever. Either way you need clear direction and goals. Write a business plan for your life. I bet you never thought of that. Imagine having a mission statement, financial plan and annual goals for YOUR life. I say get to it!

The final step is to get the help you need. To eliminate your fear, stop being so relaxed about your purpose. Get to it, either work your way to the top, get a mentor, hire a coach or do what works for you. You certainly can get great ideas and insight from others informally, but why would you just want to mimic someone else. Be authentically you! No one is good at everything, so don't be too shy to ask for help.

Days Nineteen-Twenty Assignment

Identify 5 top obstacles that you may face and write down solutions.

Obstacle	Solution
Ex. I don't have the time to start my venture.	I can stay off of social media or watch television for one hour less each week until I write out my twelve step plan. I will use FREE Time Management tools, like phone calendars.

Use this space to journal about the remake. Make it as interesting as possible. This is important, because you will have re-written your life. Soon, positive memories will replace the other ones.

_____

_____

_____

_____

_____

_____

_____

_____

_____

_____

10 HANDCUFF KEY

Days Twenty One- Twenty two

Challenge: *You are challenged to honor your uniqueness.*

The beautiful thing about walking in your purpose is that you get to really help someone else, someone who is in need of your help. Think of the world as one huge ball made from rubber bands. Then imagine that you are one of the rubber bands. If you never stretch and expand yourself, the other rubber bands can't connect. Of course there will always be a little drama in your dreams. Everyone has some issues, but think of the higher calling on your life.

Undo all the unwanted things that have ever happened to you. Identify them and get rid of them. Write them down, make a song about them or do whatever you need to release. Then identify what was consistent and unconditional. What carried you through the rough spots? Who has always supported you? Call upon it or them and give notice that you are about to blow their minds. Tell them that you will be walking in your purpose from hence forward. Understand that you were chosen, God and the universe zoned in on you, because you were special. You needed drama in order to dream.

Identify your needs. Are you only in need of love, respect and friendship or do you also need happiness and success; your needs will always have a direct connection to your natural talents. For instance, speakers need an audience, a photographer needs an object or person to photograph and everyone needs to serve their purpose. While identifying your needs, de-clutter and get rid of things that are no longer necessary. Stop self loathing and waddling in self pity; get rid of mental baggage and stop weighing yourself down. This will move you closer to serving your true purpose.

Days Twenty One- Twenty Two Assignment

Create a new you.

I am getting rid of,

1.

2.

3.

I am gaining,

1.

2.

3.

I am unique because,

1.

2.

3.

Use this space to journal about the remake. Make it as interesting as possible. This is important, because you will have re-written your life. Soon, positive memories will replace the other ones.

_____

_____

_____

_____

_____

_____

_____

_____

_____

_____

_____

_____

_____

_____

_____

_____

_____

_____

_____

_____

_____

11 Nolle Prosequi

Days Twenty Three- Twenty Four

Challenge: *You are challenged to forgive and celebrate.*

Congratulations! You are just about done. This final phase requires you to forgive and then celebrate. By now, you should be aware of what things have haunted you and are hindering you from having the life that you not only deserve, but the life that is waiting for you. The bottom line is that you must forgive in order to move on. You must forgive to free yourself from bondage. As long as you harbor hate, your eliminate room for love. Miraculously once you forgive, you will instantly feel renewed and ready to celebrate. You would have given yourself permission to live every day out loud!

Excerpt

The five essential keys to extreme happiness are (1) to honor your uniqueness, (2) empower others, (3) complete the self-work, (4) set goals that stretch you constantly, and (5) forgive. With these things in mind, be the GPS of your own life. Stop playing victim and start winning. If you needed a push, I just gave you one. Find the strength my mother found when she left. Remember me at thirteen, pretty much on my own, but still doing it. In other words, you can't just fake your way to your best self. I actually don't like the phrase "fake it till you make it." I prefer that you invest in a coach that will guide you, a mentor that will support you. Surround yourself by other leaders who are equally driven and become very protective about what you allow inside your ear space and mind. Likewise, allow good things to happen for you. Create a special place for them. Listen inward and express outward. Remember you are in control of everything that you allow in. Stand up and ask for what you want and go get it!

Answer these questions,

Who has wronged you?

Who are you forgiving?

Who do you need to forgive you?

What makes you happy?

Use this space to journal about the remake. Make it as interesting as possible. This is important, because you will have re-written your life. Soon, positive memories will replace the other ones.

_____

_____

_____

_____

_____

_____

_____

_____

_____

_____

_____

Afterword

The past, the present, and the now are all related and connected to each other. As we grow we adopt this idea that the past is no longer relevant. But that belief is wrong and something that was conditioned in our minds. Each phases of life is like a puzzle, an enigma, a riddle, and a brainteaser that's meant to teach a lesson. What lesson? How adulthood is affected by childhood and what we do is a reaction from it. Now, that reaction can be verbal, but most of the time it's physical through action. Caprice Smith shares what it was like for her growing up. Some of the good, some of the bad, and some of the ugly, but she also gives direct indications on how to beat the odds. Unfortunately, we all had unpleasant experiences growing up and we will continue as long as we live. But in no way should we use that as a crutch to not find purpose. Smith informs her readers and clients that life struggles are inevitable. However, those same struggles shape the great person you can be. But the key is being cognizant of the lessons that will come from your struggles. Smith shared vulnerable segments of her life not for sympathy, compassion, or awes, but to enlighten her readers on their potentials, their abilities, and their possibilities if the past is understood and respected. I believe having a struggled past makes the best life coaches, motivators, cheerleaders, and promoters of all things possible. Smith is a walking, talking, and living example of all things possible.

Author Pebbles D. Armwood

Pebbles Armwood Presents Mental Fitness LLC.

ABOUT THE AUTHOR

The author, high impact mindset trainer and transformational power house Caprice Smith is an Empowering Business Coach and a highly sought after speaker. She has been named 2010 Top 100 Minority Business In The Mid-Atlantic Region and Baltimore's Best. She also won 1st runner up in the 2013 Mrs. Corporate America Pageant.

Smith founded SharperMinds Consultants, a non-profit 501c3, and has helped many women to find their voices. Coaching comes very natural to her and her unique style yields result. Her clients are blown away as they discover their own purposes. She has delivered her signature speech, 5 Steps to Extreme Happiness & Keys To Access Your Inner Entrepreneur to diverse audiences.

She uses her experience in the interrogation room as a detective in a major metropolitan city; where she has spent several years face to face with sexual predators and abusers. She aggressively teaches others about their power, their purpose and latent things that hold them from greatness. Smith holds a Masters in Education from the University of Maryland, University College and a Bachelors in Psychology from Coppin State University. She is a wife, a mother, and an active member of her community. She accepts her role as a mentor, role model and leader.

She authored Uncuffed~Behind My Smile and The Art of Listening, An Effective Guide To Listening, which has been given five stars by readers. She also developed the learning curriculum called the ShArPI Model which has been taught in the Baltimore School System and organizations throughout Maryland. Smith is named among top world renowned coaches in the collaboration, Authentic Business Revolution E-Book with Rebecca Matia's team. Ultimately she teaches you how to change your way of thinking, how a Change of Mind will Change Your Life!

Smith challenges everyone, especially women to uncover their purpose and take the first step toward a more powerful living, by taking The 24 Day Challenge To Living Uncuffed.

He who began a good work in you, will be faithful to complete it.

Philippians 1:6

18652092R00076

Made in the USA
Middletown, DE
14 March 2015